You Laugh You Lose Challenge

300 Jokes for Kids That Are Funny, Silly, And Interactive Fun the Whole Family Will Love

7-Year-Old Edition

You Laugh You Lose Series Volume 2

~With Illustrations for Kids~

Smiley Beagle

ISBN: 9798633915037

Table of Contents

Introduction

We wrote this book to make you laugh. We love making people laugh, and we know that you, your family, and your friends will love it too! We especially want you to love our jokes! We want you to tell them everywhere you go! Wherever you think people could use a good laugh. Leave them rolling on the ground, make them cry and beg, and always leave them asking for more.

Sharing laughter is the best thing about telling a joke, and once one person starts, everyone joins in. So, be the joke starter and bring laughs and smiles to everyone you know.

Rules

Each player takes turns reading one joke from the book. If somebody laughs, then the person reading it gets a point. Then the book is given to the next player, and it is their turn to read.

Smiling at the joke doesn't count, but any sort of laughing is worth 1 point. The first person to reach 7 points wins! Feel free to play with as many people as you want or even form teams to make funny faces to try and get everyone in on the laughing.

Remember to be fair and always admit if you laugh, games with arguments are no fun. And the most important thing of all is to laugh as much as you can!

Going Solo

Want to try to beat the "You Laugh You Lose" challenge on your own? Think you got what it takes to beat one of the funniest books around? Go on; we dare you!

See how far you can get without cracking up! When you are done, use the ranking system below to gauge your score.

10 jokes – A Jester, At Best!

25 jokes – The Town Clown!

50 jokes – Passable Prankster!

100 jokes – Chuckle Champion!

150 jokes – Wisecrack Wizard!

200 jokes – Ha-Ha Hero!

300 jokes – Laugh Legend!

Chapter One
Knock-Knock Jokes

1. Knock, knock.

Who's there?

Handsome.

Handsome who?

Ah, handsome pizza to me, please!

2. Knock, knock.

Who's there?

Razor.

Razor who?

Razor hands, this is a stick-up!

3. Knock, knock.

Who's there?

Joe King.

Joe King who?

Joe King with you is too much fun!

4. Knock, knock.

Who's there?

Rhino.

Rhino who?

Well, Rhino every knock-knock joke there is!

5. Knock, knock.

Who's there?

Turnip.

Turnip who?

Well, turnip the volume, it's too quiet!

6. Knock, knock.

Who's there?

Cash.

Cash who?

I knew you were a nut!

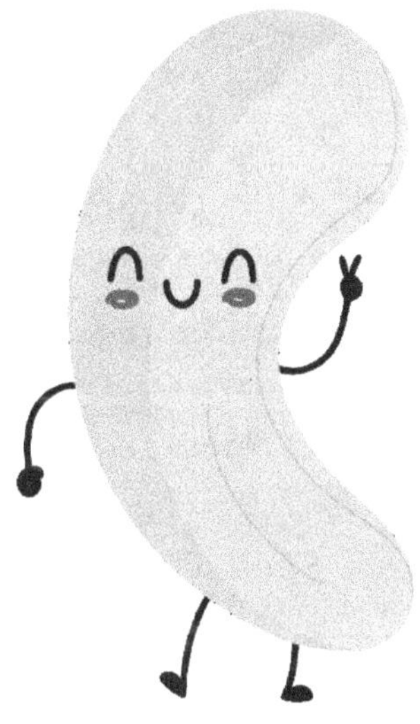

7. Knock, knock.

Who's there?

Doris.

Doris who?

Doris locked, that's why I'm knocking!

8. Knock, knock.

Who's there?

Spell.

Spell who?

W-H-O!

9. Knock, knock.

Who's there?

Alpaca.

Alpaca who?

Well, alpaca the suitcase, you load up the car!

10. Knock, knock.

Who's there?

A herd.

A herd who?

Well, a herd you were home, so I came over!

11. Knock, knock.

Who's there?

Dozen.

Dozen who?

Well, dozen anyone want to let me in?

12. Knock, knock.

Who's there?

Tank.

Tank who?

You're welcome!

13. Knock, knock.

Who's there?

Figs.

Figs who?

Figs the doorbell, it's broken!

14. Knock, knock.

Who's there?

Cows.

Cows who?

No, owls who! Cows moo!

15. Knock, knock.

Who's there?

Woo.

Woo who?

Don't get so excited, it's just a joke!

16. Knock, knock.

Who's there?

Oven.

Oven who?

Oven thinking of you!

17. Knock, knock.

Who's there?

Stopwatch.

Stopwatch who?

Stopwatch you're doing and open this door!

18. Knock, knock.

Who's there?

Ben.

Ben who?

Ben knocking for 10 minutes!

19. Knock, knock.

Who's there?

Iva.

Iva who?

Iva sore hand from knocking!

20. Knock, knock.

Who's there?

Needle.

Needle who?

I needle little money for the movies!

Chapter Two

Body Jokes

1. Which teeth do you have to brush?

The ones you want to keep!

2. Why are robots never afraid?

They have nerves of steel!

3. What did the nose say to the finger?

Quit picking on me!

4. What has two legs but can't walk?

A pair of pants!

5. What can you hold without using your hands?

Your breath!

6. What do you call an alien with three eyes?

An aliiien!

7. Why didn't the girl tell the doctor that she ate some glue?

Her lips were sealed!

8. I don't think I need a spine.

It's just holding me back!

9. Why is your nose in the middle of your face?

Because it is the scenter!

10. What do you do when you break your toe?

Call the toe truck!

11. What has four eyes but no face?

Mississippi!

12. What has one head, one foot, and four legs?

A bed!

13. What's as big as you but weighs nothing?

Your shadow!

14. Why can't your nose be 12 inches long?

Because then it would be a foot!

15. What kind of button won't do anything when you press it?

A bellybutton!

16. What has arms and legs, but no head?

A chair!

17. How did the person feel after they ate a pillow?

Down in the mouth!

18. What do you say when you meet a two-headed person?

Hello! Hello!

Chapter Three

Food Jokes

1. Why did the doughnut go to the dentist?

For a filling!

2. Why did the cookie go to the hospital?

Because he felt crummy!

3. What does bread do on vacation?

Loaf around!

4. What did the banana say to the dog?

Nothing! Bananas can't talk!

5. What is a computer's favorite snack?

Computer chips!

6. What kind of nut has no shell?

A doughnut!

7. What kind of cheese is not yours?

Nacho cheese!

8. What do you call a mean sandwich?

Rude food!

9. What do you do if someone thinks an onion is the only food that can make them cry?

Throw a coconut at their face!

10. What do you call a jelly bean found on the beach?

Sandy candy!

11. What is a calendar's favorite food?

Dates!

12. What does the toast wear to bed?

Jammies!

13. How do they serve smart hamburgers?

On honor rolls!

14. What is a boxer's favorite drink?

Punch!

15. Why did the orange stop in the middle of the hill?

It ran out of juice!

16. Why did the kid go to Minnesota?

To get a mini soda!

17. Why do we put candles on the top of a birthday cake?

Because it's too hard to put them on the bottom!

18. What type of bagel can fly?

A plain bagel!

19. What's the difference between mashed potatoes and pea soup?

Anyone can mash potatoes!

20. If you had eight apples in one hand and five apples in the other, what would you have?

Really big hands!

21. What kind of meals do math teachers eat?

Square meals!

22. What do snowmen like to eat for breakfast?

A frosted doughnut!

23. What is a cheerleader's favorite drink?

Root beer!

24. What is a scarecrow's favorite fruit?

Straw-berries!

25. What does a sick lemon need?

Lemon aid!

26. Why did the melon jump into the lake?

It wanted to be a water-melon.

27. Did you hear about the restaurant on the moon?

The food is good, but there's no atmosphere!

28. Why is a baseball team similar to a muffin?

They both depend on the batter!

29. Two olives on a fence, one falls off. The other one calls down, "Are you okay?"

"Olive." (I'll live)

30. Why did the man eat the candle?

He wanted a light snack!

31. What kind of key opens a banana?

A monkey!

32. What do you call artificial spaghetti?

Mockaroni!

33. What happens to a hamburger that misses a lot of school?

He has a lot of ketchup time!

34. How do you make a hot dog stand?

Steal its chair!

35. What did the banana say to the monkey?

Nothing, bananas can't talk!

Chapter Four
People Jokes

1. What time should you go to the dentist?

Tooth-hurty!

2. What day of the week are most twins born on?

Twos-day!

3. Who do you call when the ocean needs a little cleaning?

A mermaid!

4. Where do people in Antarctica get their hair cut?

At the brrr-brrr shop!

5. What do you call people who love ceilings?

Ceiling fans!

6. Where does a scientist wizard work?

In a labracadabratory!

7. Why was King Arthur's army too tired to fight?

It had too many sleepless knights!

8. Why did the carpenter fall asleep on the job?

He was board!

9. Why did the spy stay in bed?

Because he was under cover!

10. Who makes the best cake on a baseball team?

The batter!

11. Why did the baseball player bring a rope to the game?

Because he wanted to tie the score!

12. Why was the baseball player arrested in the middle of the game?

He was caught stealing second base!

13. Why was the vacationing doctor so mad?

He had no patients!

14. When are kids most likely to go to school?

When the door is open!

15. Why did the gardener plant his money?

He wanted his soil to be rich!

16. What is an astronaut's favorite key on the keyboard?

The space bar!

17. A man is washing his car with his son.

The son asks, "Dad, can't you just use a sponge?"

18. What has 18 legs and catches flies?

A baseball team!

19. Where do astronauts keep their sandwiches?

In a launch box!

20. How much does it cost a pirate to get his ears pierced?

About a buck an ear!

21. Why couldn't the athlete listen to her music?

Because she broke the record!

22. What do postal workers do when they're mad?

They stamp their feet!

23. What nails do carpenters hate to hit?

Fingernails!

24. Why did the singer climb a ladder?

She wanted to reach the high notes!

25. Customer: Do you have spaghetti on the menu today?

Waiter: No, l cleaned it off.

26. Where do superheroes shop?

At the supermarket!

27. What is a cheerleader's favorite color?

Yeller!

28. Why was the clown sad?

She broke her funny bone!

29. What kind of shoes do all spies wear?

Sneakers!

30. Did you hear the one about the human cannonball?

He was hired and fired in the same night!

31. What is the difference between a school teacher and a train?

The teacher says, "spit your gum out!" and the train says, "chew, chew, chew!"

32. Why did the soccer player bring string to the game?

So that he could tie the score!

33. What kind of bed does a mermaid sleep in?

A water bed!

34. What kind of crackers do firemen like in their soup?

Firecrackers!

35. What kind of cake do you bring to the dentist's office?

A tooth-cake!

36. Who sits on babies?

A babysitter!

37. Why did the baker stop making doughnuts?

He got fed up with the hole business!

38. What do farmers give their wives on Valentine's Day?

Hogs and Kisses!

39. Why are there old dinosaur bones in the museum?

Because the curator can't afford new ones!

Chapter Five

Animal Jokes

1. What type of markets do dogs avoid?

Flea markets!

2. Why should you not let a bear operate the remote?

He will keep pressing the paws button!

3. Why do birds fly?

It's faster than walking.

4. What do ants get when they do all their chores?

An allow-ants!

5. What's a firefly's favorite game?

Hide-and-glow-seek!

6. What kind of party do snails have?

A shell-ebration!

7. What do you call a phony serpent?

A fake snake!

8. What do you call a classy fish?

Sofishticated!

9. What do you get when you cross a porcupine and a turtle?

A slowpoke!

10. What do you get when you cross a fly, a car, and a dog?

A flying carpet!

11. What do you get when you cross a fish with an elephant?

Swimming trunks!

12. What do fish take to stay healthy?

Vitamin sea!

13. What has four legs, a trunk, and sunglasses?

A mouse on vacation!

14. How do you keep a skunk from smelling?

Plug its nose!

15. How do you get a dog to stop digging in the garden?

Take away his shovel!

16. How does a mouse feel after it takes a shower?

Squeaky clean!

17. What do you call an elephant in a phone booth?

Stuck!

18. What is a cheetah's favorite thing to eat?

Fast food!

19. How do you stop a dog barking in the back seat of a car?

Put him in the front seat!

20. How do you make a goldfish old?

Take away the g!

21. What do you call a cow that eats your grass?

A lawn moo-er!

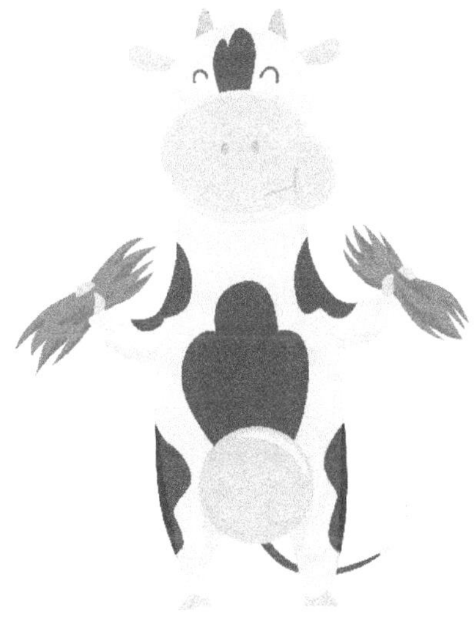

22. Where do mice park their boats?

At the hickory dickory dock!

23. What is a butterfly's favorite subject at school?

Mothematics!

24. What's the biggest moth in the world?

A mammoth!

25. Why do hummingbirds hum?

They forgot the words!

26. What did the Dalmatian say after lunch?

That hit the spot!

27. What's a cow's favorite holiday?

Moo Year's Eve!

28. Why do porcupines always win the game?

They have the most points!

29. When does a horse talk?

Whinney wants to!

30. What do you give a sick bird?

Tweetment!

31. What animal has more lives than a cat?

Frogs, they croak every night!

32. What kind of bird works at a construction site?

The crane!

33. What creature is smarter than a talking parrot?

A spelling bee!

34. Why don't bats live alone?

They like to hang out with their friends!

35. When can three giant dinosaurs get under an umbrella and not get wet?

When it's not raining!

36. Why did the bee go to the doctor?

Because she had hives!

37. Why do fish live in saltwater?

Because pepper makes them sneeze!

38. What do you call a camel with no humps?

Humphrey!

39. What's long, green, and goes "hith"?

A snake that bit their tongue!

40. What snakes are found on cars?

Windshield vipers!

41. Why do penguins carry fish in their beaks?

Because they don't have any pockets!

42. How do you know if there's an elephant under your bed?

Your head hits the ceiling!

43. How do you keep an elephant from charging?

Take away her charging cable!

44. Why couldn't the pony sing in the choir?

Because she was a little horse!

45. Where does the chicken like to eat?

At a roosterant!

46. Why did the dog do so well in school?

Because he was the teacher's pet!

47. Why do cows wear bells?

Because their horns don't work!

48. Two toothpicks are standing by the side of the road when a hedgehog walks by.

One toothpick says to the other one, "oh no! We missed our bus!"

49. Do you know what goes through a bug's mind right before it hits the windshield?

His Butt!

50. What sound does a lip-less sheep make?

Aaaaaaaaaaaaaahh!

51. What do you get when you cross an elephant with a kangaroo?

Big holes all over Australia!

52. What's the difference between a termite and a refrigerator?

One eats the houses and the other houses the eats!

53. Where do you park your dog at night?

In a barking lot!

54. What do termites eat for breakfast?

Oakmeal!

55. What do you call a crate of ducks?

A box of quackers!

56. What do you call a bear with no socks on?

Bare-foot!

57. What do you do with a blue whale?

Try to cheer him up!

58. What does a shark eat with peanut butter?

Jellyfish!

59. Do skunks celebrate Valentine's Day?

Sure, they're very scent-imental!

60. Why was the pelican kicked out of the hotel?

Because he had a big bill!

61. Where do bulls get their messages?

On a bull-etin board!

62. Why did the shark cross the ocean?

To get to the other tide!

63. What do polar bears eat for lunch?

Ice berg-ers!

64. What do you get if you cross a teddy bear with a pig?

A teddy boar!

65. What bird is with you at every meal?

A swallow!

66. What do you get if you cross a canary and a 50-foot long snake?

A sing-a-long!

67. What kind of cats like to go bowling?

Alley cats!

68. Lily: I'd like to buy some birdseed.

Bruno: How many birds do you have?

Lily: None! I want to grow some!

69. What are caterpillars afraid of?

Doger-pillars!

70. Why didn't the boy believe the tiger?

He thought it was a lion!

71. What do you call a grumpy cow?

Moo-dy!

72. What happened to the lost cattle?

Nobody's herd!

73. What should you do if you find a dinosaur in your bed?

Find somewhere else to sleep!

74. What happened when the dinosaur took the train home?

She had to bring it back!

75. Why was the dinosaur afraid of the ocean?

Because there was something fishy about it!

76. What makes more noise than a dinosaur?

Two dinosaurs!

77. What was the scariest prehistoric animal?

The Terror-dactyl!

78. Why are dinosaurs extinct?

Because they wouldn't take a bath!

79. What do you call a dinosaur that left its armor out in the rain?

A Stegosau-rust!

80. What do you call a dinosaur that never gives up?

Try-Try-Try-ceratops!

81. Where did Velociraptor buy things?

At a dino-store!

82. How do dinosaurs pay their bills?

With Tyrannosaurus checks!

83. What do you get when you cross a dinosaur with fireworks?

Dino-mite!

84. Do you know how long dinosaurs should be fed?

Exactly the same as short dinosaurs!

85. Why did the snowman call his dog "Frost"?

Because Frost-bites!

86. When is a black dog not a black dog?

When it's a greyhound!

87. What do you get if you cross a cocker spaniel, a poodle, and a rooster?

Cockerpoodledoo!

88. What do you get if you cross a frog and a dog?

A croaker spaniel!

89. How do fleas travel from place to place?

By itch-hiking!

90. Why do you get if you cross a chili pepper, a shovel, and a terrier?

A hot-diggity-dog!

91. Did you hear about the dog that had puppies on the side of the road?

She got a ticket for littering!

92. Which fish is the most famous?

The star fish!

93. How deep is a frog pond?

Kneedeep, kneedeep!

94. What does a frog say when it washes a window?

Rub it, rub it, rub it!

95. What type of horses only go out at night?

Nightmares!

96. What does it mean if you find a horseshoe on the road?

Some poor horse is walking around in his socks!

97. What sickness do horses hate the most?

Hay fever!

98. How do monkeys get down the stairs?

They slide down the banana-ster!

99. What do you call a monkey with a banana in each ear?

Anything you want, it can't hear you!

100. Where do hamsters come from?

Hamsterdam!

101. Someone said you sounded like an owl.

Who?

102. Why did the owl say, "Tweet, tweet"?

Because she didn't give a hoot!

103. What do you get when you cross a parrot and a shark?

A bird that talks your ear off!

104. Why do monkeys like bananas?

Because they have appeal!

105. Where do penguins go to dance?

The snow ball!

106. How does a penguin make pancakes?

With its flippers!

107. Who's the penguin's favorite Aunt?

Aunt-Arctica!

Chapter Six

A Little Bit 'o' Everything

Jokes

1. What did one penny say to another penny?

Together, we make cents!

2. How do mountains stay warm in the winter?

Snowcaps!

3. Why are teddy bears never hungry?

They are always stuffed!

4. Why do scissors always win a race?

Because they take a shortcut!

5. Where do rocks like to sleep?

Bedrock!

6. Why isn't there a clock in the library?

Because it tocks too much!

7. What does every birthday end with?

The letter Y!

8. What kind of music scares balloons?

Pop Music!

9. Lily: What are you doing under there?

Bruno: Under where?

Lily: Ha-ha! You said underwear!

10. What time is it when the clock strikes 13?

Time to get a new clock!

11. What do you call two friends on a boat?

Friendship!

12. Why did the man put his money in the freezer?

He wanted cold, hard cash!

13. How do you talk to a giant?

Use big words!

14. What has four wheels and flies?

A garbage truck!

15. What do you call a medieval lamp?

Knight light!

16. What word has five letters and starts with "gas"?

Truck!

17. Where does the water go when you boil it?

No idea, but it'll be mist!

18. What did the beach say as the tide came in?

Long time, no sea!

19. Did you hear about the guy who got hit on the head with a can of soda?

He was lucky it was a soft drink!

20. Want to hear something terrible?

Paper! I told you it was tear-able!

21. What did one blade of grass say to another about the lack of rain?

I guess we'll just have to make dew!

22. Bruno: How did you get hit on the head with a book?

Lily: I only have my shelf to blame!

23. How do you make a rock float?

Put it in a glass with some ice cream and root beer!

24. After each sentence below, say, "my friend did too."

I went to the circus.

I ate some popcorn.

I went on some rides.

I ate some cotton candy.

I got some balloons.

I got some more to eat.

The balloons popped...

My friend did too!

25. Where do cars go for a swim?

At the carpool!

26. Why did the drum take a nap?

It was beat!

27. Where do all the letters sleep?

In the alphabed!

28. Why did the tree go to the dentist?

It needed a root canal!

29. Tom: I bet I can make you say purple.

Joe: How?

Tom: What colors are in the American flag?

Joe: Red, white, and blue.

Tom: I told you I can make you say red.

Joe: You said purple!

Tom: I told you I could make you say purple!

30. Why did the boy take a ruler to bed?

To see how long he slept!

31. What do you get if you cross a fridge and a stereo?

Cool music!

32. What do you call a story about a broken pencil?

Pointless!

33. What can you put in a barrel to make it lighter?

Holes!

34. What washes up on very small beaches?

Microwaves!

35. Why wasn't the girl sad when her flashlight battery died?

Because she was de-lighted!

36. What is the shortest month?

May, because it has only three letters!

37. What's the biggest problem with snow boots?

They melt!

38. What did the tornado say to the sports car?

Want to go for a spin?

39. Why did the girl sit on a clock?

To be on time!

40. What did the baseball glove say to the baseball?

Catch you later!

41. Two waves had a race. Who won?

They tide!

42. Why is tennis such a loud sport?

The players raise a racquet!

43. Why did the man run around his bed?

Because he was trying to catch up on his sleep!

44. Who says sticks and stones may break my bones, but words will never hurt me?

A guy who has never been hit with a dictionary!

45. Why did Grandma put wheels on her rocking chair?

So that she could rock 'n' roll!

46. How do you get straight A's?

By using a ruler!

47. What did the little boy's mom say when he asked her to buy him shoes for gym?

"Tell Jim to buy his own shoes."

48. How do you cut a wave in half?

You use a sea saw!

49. What kind of shorts do clouds wear?

Thunderwear!

50. What's brown and sticky?

A stick!

51. What is the best time of year to jump on a trampoline?

Spring time!

52. What is brown, hairy, and wears sunglasses?

A coconut on vacation!

53. What do you call a fast fungus?

A mush-vroom!

54. Lettuce, an egg, and a faucet had a race. What was the result?

The lettuce came in ahead, the egg got beat, and the faucet is still running!

55. Why don't they make pencils with erasers on both ends?

That would be pointless!

56. When does it rain money?

When there is a "change" in the weather!

57. **What did the big flower say to the small flower?**

What's up, bud?

58. **Where can you always find money?**

In the dictionary!

59. **Why did the two 4's skip lunch?**

They already 8!

60. **Why did the student do multiplication problems on the floor?**

The teacher told her not to use tables!

61. **What room is useless for a ghost?**

A living room!

62. **When is a door not a door?**

When it's ajar!

63. **What should you take on a trip to the desert?**

A thirst-aid kit!

64. **How do trees get on the internet?**

They log in!

65. What can you catch but not throw?

A cold!

66. What did one hat say to the other?

Stay here, I'm going on ahead!

67. What's the worst thing about throwing a party in space?

You have to planet!

68. Why was the belt arrested?

It was holding up some pants!

69. What musical instrument is found in the bathroom?

A tube-a toothpaste!

70. Where do library books like to sleep?

Under their covers!

71. Why can't a bicycle stand up by itself?

Because it's two-tired!

72. What did one wall say to the other?

Meet you at the corner!

73. Why did the man sleep under his car?

Because he wanted to wake up oily in the morning!

74. What has one horn and gives milk?

A milk truck!

75. What letters are not in the alphabet?

The ones in the mail, of course!

76. How do you make a bandstand?

Take away their chairs!

77. What did the ground say to the earthquake?

You crack me up!

78. Why did the worker put a clock under their desk?

Because they wanted to work over-time!

79. When is a car not a car?

When it turns into a garage!

80. Why did the little boy put lipstick on his forehead?

He wanted to make up his mind!

81. What did the pencil sharpener say to the pencil?

Stop going in circles and get to the point!

Conclusion

We hope you and your family enjoyed our whole heaping book full of jokes. But if that still wasn't enough for you, then we suggest checking out the other joke books that we have available.

Also, if you are up for the challenge, we have a book of riddles for the kids and adults alike!

We hope that your days are filled with fun and funnies, and we hope that we will get to laugh together again very soon.

Up For A Challenge?!?

Get updates on new releases and exclusive offers sent straight to your inbox! Sign up for Smiley Beagle's newsletter and you can also receive a FREE copy of "Difficult Riddles For Kids" today.

Thank you, and see you soon.

Sign up by scanning the QR code below with your phone's default camera app.